FIFTH HARM⑤NY

The dream begins ...now!

W

FRANKLIN WATTS

LONDON•SYDNEY

First published in 2013 by
Franklin Watts
338 Euston Road
London NW1 3BH

Franklin Watts Australia
Level 17/207 Kent Street
Sydney NSW 2000

Editor: Adrian Cole
Art direction: Peter Scoulding
Project managed and created by Dynamo Limited
    Author: Hettie Bingham
    Design and layout: Dynamo Limited

Acknowledgements:

Cover: Fox/Getty Images, Endpaper: Ben Horton/Getty Images, p1: John Lamparski/Getty Images
p3: Fox/Getty Images, p4: Fox/Getty Images, p5: Fox/Getty Images, p6: Fox/Getty Images, p7: Helga Esteb/Shutterstock,
p8: s_bukley/Shutterstock, p9: Fox/Getty Images, Helga Esteb/Shutterstock, p10: Charles Norfleet/Getty Images,
Featureflash/Shutterstock, Callahan/Shutterstock, Alex Luengo/Shutterstock, p11: Startraks Photo/Rex Images,
p12/13: Helga Esteb/Shutterstock, Africa Studio/Shutterstock, p14: Helga Esteb/Shutterstock - p15: Michael N. Todaro/
Getty Images, Ruslan Kudrin/Shutterstock, Anna Vishnevskaya/Shutterstock, p16: Helga Esteb/Shutterstock, Featureflash/
Shutterstock, p17: Fox/Getty Images, Helga Esteb/Shutterstock, Featureflash/Shutterstock, Debby Wong/Shutterstock,
p18: Joe Kohen/Getty Images, Callahan/Shutterstock, Alex Luengo/Shutterstock, p19: Startraks Photo/Rex Images,
p20: Startraks Photo/Rex Images, Ben Horton/Getty Images, p21: anyamuse/Shutterstock, Mr.Reborn55/Shutterstock,
Helga Esteb/Shutterstock, p22: Fox/Getty Images, Startraks Photo/Rex Images, Helga Esteb/Shutterstock, Featureflash/
Shutterstock, landmarkmedia/Shutterstock, p23: Startraks Photo/Rex Images, s_bukley/Shutterstock, Helga Esteb/
Shutterstock, Featureflash/Shutterstock, p24/25: Fox/Getty Images, p26: Charles Norfleet/Getty Images, Callahan/
Shutterstock, Alex Luengo/Shutterstock, p27: Startraks Photo/Rex Images, p28/29 Slaven Vlasic/Getty Images,
p30: Ilya S. Savenok/Getty Images, p31: Fox/Getty Images, anyamuse/Shutterstock, Mr.Reborn55/Shutterstock,
p32: Maridav/Shutterstock, giorgiomtb/Shutterstock, s_bukley/Shutterstock, David Davis/Shutterstock, Featureflash/
Shutterstock, p33: s_bukley/Shutterstock, Danomyte/Shutterstock, p34: John Lamparski/Getty Images, Callahan/
Shutterstock, Alex Luengo/Shutterstock, p35: Startraks Photo/Rex Images, p36/37: Helga Esteb/Shutterstock, sabri deniz
kizil/Shutterstock, p38: Joe Seer/Shutterstock, p39: Rachel Murray/Getty Images, Africa Studio/Shutterstock, Michael C.
Gray/Shutterstock, p40/41: Joe Seer/Shutterstock, p42: Callahan/Shutterstock, Alex Luengo/Shutterstock, Helga Esteb/
Shutterstock, p43: Startraks Photo/Rex Images, p44/45: John Lamparski//Getty Images, p46: Helga Esteb/Shutterstock,
p47: Dimitry Atanasov/Shutterstock, Elnur/Shutterstock, Taylor Hill/Getty Images, p48: Owen Sweeney/Invision/AP/PAI,
D Dipasupil/Getty Images, Endpaper: Slaven Vlasic/Getty Images

A CIP catalogue record for this book
is available from the British Library.

ISBN: 978 1 4451 2690 6

Printed in China

Franklin Watts is a division of Hachette
Children's Books, an Hachette UK company.
www.hachette.co.uk

CONTENTS

PERFECT HARMONY
The dream begins ...now!

> "I knew from the girls' first performance at the Judges' Homes in Miami that we'd done the right thing." Simon Cowell

5H originally auditioned for *The X Factor* (US – Season Two) as solo artists, but some things are just meant to be. The judges could see that these were five talented young ladies and made the inspired decision to put them together.

With voices that blend so beautifully, these girls sound as if they've been singing together all their lives!

Five great singers:

Dinah Jane Hansen
Ally Brooke
Camila Cabello
Normani Kordei
Lauren Jauregui

The band wasn't always called Fifth Harmony. When the girls made their first appearance on *The X Factor* as a girl group, they went by the name of **LYLAS** (Love You Like a Sister). Next they tried out the name **1432** (I love you two). This did not go down well with Simon Cowell, who hated the name – back to square one! The American audience was given the challenge to find a new name and they came up with **Fifth Harmony**.

TOGETHER THEY ARE
FIFTH HARMONY

THE X FACTOR STORY

They're big stars now, but how did it all begin for 5H?

Normani

Normani Kordei belts out a version of Aretha Franklin's *Chain of Fools* and shows the judges just why she deserves her place at Bootcamp.

Camila

Camila Cabello sings *Respect* for her audition piece. Her performance blows the judges away and secures her place at Bootcamp.

Ally

Ally Brooke sings *On My Knees* by Jaci Velasquez for her audition piece. She also gets to Bootcamp with four big 'easy breezy yeses'.

Dinah

Dinah Jane Hansen auditions with the Beyoncé hit, *If I Were a Boy*. It gets her four 'yeses' and a place at Bootcamp.

Lauren

Lauren Jauregui makes it to Bootcamp with four 'yeses' after her 'husky' and powerful performance of Alicia Keys' *If I Ain't Got You*.

BOOTCAMP

There are tears when the girls think it's the end of the road after being eliminated from Bootcamp as solo artists... but wait! The judges call the girls back on stage and give them the chance to perform as a group at the 'Judges' Homes' round.

JUDGES' HOMES

Now together as a new girl group named LYLAS, the girls impress Simon with their version of Shontelle's *Impossible*. "That was unbelievable... I don't know what I expected but it's gone somewhere else," says Simon. Not so impossible after all, then!

Everyone can see that they are a perfect combination. It's history in the making!

THE X FACTOR
STORY

LIVE SHOWS

➤ Week one:

With the new name 1432, the girls perform *We Are Never Getting Back Together* by Taylor Swift. On the results show they have to perform Demi Lovato's *Skyscraper* in a sing-off with Sister-C. They make it through – yay!

➤ Week two:

Now named Fifth Harmony, they sing Christina Perri's *A Thousand Years* from the movie *The Twilight Saga: Breaking Dawn*. The performance gets the judges' approval; Britney Spears tells them they "shined the whole way". Simon says he "couldn't be more proud". On the results show, 5H make fifth place – well done, girls!

➤ Week three:

For 'Diva Week' 5H pick Mariah Carey – who else?! Their performance of *Hero* makes sixth place. It's going great!

➤ Week four:

On the Thanksgiving-themed show, the girls dedicate their performance to God and their families. Their version of *I'll Stand by You* by The Pretenders puts them in seventh place. We're standing by you, Fifth Harmony!

➤ Week five:

There's heart-breaking news for Ally when she hears that her grandfather has passed away. But the girls are right behind her and they dedicate their performance to his memory. It's a number one themed show and *Stronger (What Doesn't Kill You)* by Kelly Clarkson, puts 5H in fourth place. Ally gets a great hug from her girls at the end. Simon says, "Your grandfather would be proud of you".

➤ Week six:

The girls perform Adele's *Set Fire to the Rain* and Demi Lovato's *Give Your Heart a Break* – but they only make the bottom two. OMG! They sing for survival against Diamond White with Mariah Carey's *Any Time You Need a Friend* and land a spot in the top four. Phew!

➤ The semi-finals

The girls perform *Anything Could Happen* by Ellie Goulding, which is their most popular performance on the show. They also perform *Impossible* by Shontelle with solos in Spanish by Camila, Lauren and Ally.

➤ And finally:

The girls perform *Anything Could Happen* for the second time as their 'Song of the Series'. Next is a surprise appearance from Demi Lovato who joins 5H with a sensational performance of *Give Your Heart a Break*. "This is so much fun," says Demi. "These girls are so easy to work with." Their final song for the night is *Let It Be* by The Beatles.

Our Fab Five don't make the top two on *The X Factor*, but they're number one in our hearts! And Simon Cowell isn't going to 'let it be' – he signs the girls to his own record label.

The girls perform a farewell song – *Christmas (Baby Please Come Home)* – to the X Factor audience on part two of the finals.

But it isn't goodbye, because...

THE DREAM BEGINS
...NOW!

 # DINAH

5H PROFILE

Name: **Dinah Jane Hansen**

Born: **22nd June 1997**

Star sign: **Cancer**

Hair colour: **Brown**

Eye colour: **Dark brown**

Hometown: **Santa Ana, California**

"We want our songs to be fun, positive and inspiring, and for our vocals to shine through."
Dinah

➤ Dinah loves to sing harmonies. "It makes me feel like I'm in Destiny's Child," she says. And there was no shortage of people to practise with when she was growing up in Orange County; she shared a house with 23 family members!

➤ Dinah made her first public appearance at just 7 years old when she sang the US National Anthem in Sacramento, California.

➤ With her powerful voice and fantastic vocal range, Dinah has been compared to Beyoncé, who is one of her favourite singers.

HAIR HARMONY!

These ladies have luscious locks and they love to let it all hang loose. But how do they style their hair when they need to be red carpet-ready?

Normani

Normani opts for a sophisticated look with swept up hair. It goes perfectly with her Val Stefani dress.

Camila

Bows are a favourite look for Camila. White chiffon adds a touch of class that compliments her Sherri Hill dress perfectly.

Ally

Ally has gone for long waves – so cute with her pink dress by Sherri Hill.

Lauren

Lauren looks lovely with long, soft waves swept over one shoulder. She also wears a dress by Sherri Hill.

Dinah

Dinah has piled up her corkscrew curls, which add a twist to her glamorous silver dress by Aqua.

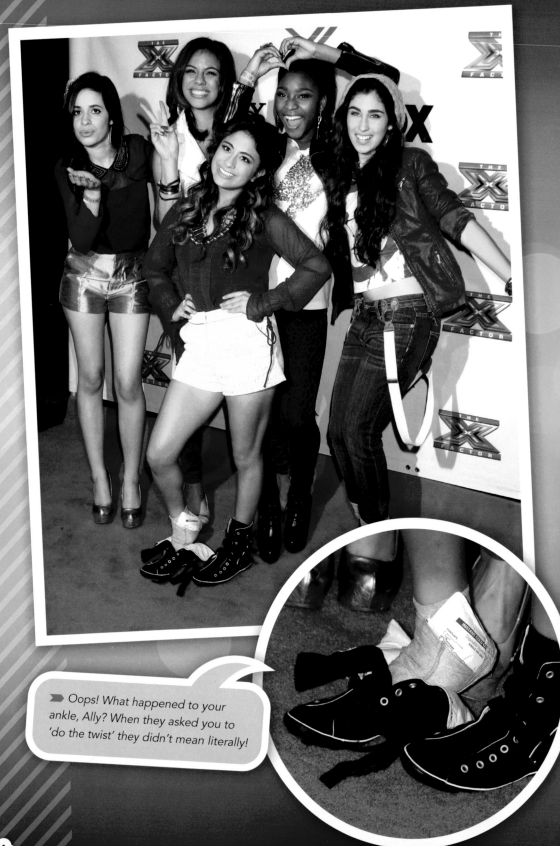

➤ Oops! What happened to your ankle, Ally? When they asked you to 'do the twist' they didn't mean literally!

LAUREN

➤ *Lauren's style:* **Hipster**

Letting it all hang loose with a rock chick vibe.

Outgoing Lauren describes herself as a bit of a hipster.

"I like to dress pretty sometimes … but with an edge," she says. **"If I put on a dress with a leather jacket, that would be me."**

➤ *Lauren's favourite accessories:*

"Definitely shoes … and rings – but mostly shoes!"

➤ *We've also noticed that...*

Lauren looks good in a hat – yep, she's got it going on up top.

➤ *Lauren also likes:*

Tassels, denim and lace!

5H PLAYLIST

"*I have my favourites ... and then I have my favourite favourites ... and then I have my old favourites ... and so on,*" says Lauren

⚑ 5H's go-to karaoke song is **Hey Now – What Dreams Are Made Of by Hilary Duff.** Camila says, "Our dream is just beginning and this song really reflects the way we feel right now."

"**Mariah Carey's *Anytime You Need a Friend*** has got to be on the list," says 5H. "The words really sum up how we feel about each other as friends."

⚑ It's no secret that 5H are all big **One Direction** fans, so it's no surprise that *Every Time We Touch* is one of their all-time favourite songs. "We love everything that One Direction does, but that song especially," says Normani.

▶ **Ellie Goulding's**
***Anything Could
Happen*** was 5H's
'Song of the Series' on
The X Factor – so that
makes it a big favourite!

◀ "When we sang **Shontelle's *Impossible***,
something clicked for me, like I started
crying because I knew, I felt it in my heart
that we were supposed to be together and
that it was meant to be," said Lauren.

Dinah's favourite song by
Ed Sheeran is *Kiss Me*.
Aw, she's a romantic at heart!

*"How do you choose your favourite
song? I mean it's so hard – there
are so many good ones!"* says Camila

♡ ALLY

5H PROFILE

Name: **Ally Brooke**

Born: **7th July 1993**

Star sign: **Cancer**

Hair colour: **Brown**

Eye colour: **Brown**

Hometown: **San Antonio, Texas**

➤ Ally was born prematurely, weighing just over 0.5 kilogram (1lb 4oz) – but she had a good pair of lungs on her and came out screaming, which is unusual for such a tiny baby. That's why her dad knew right away that she was born to sing!

➤ **"My favourite thing about being in a group is that I get to share all of this with the girls ... that's awesome!"** says Ally.

Greetings from **TEXAS** *USA*

"The songs are a direct reflection of us and what we go through. Because we've been able to co-write, we've been able to personalize our music and make it relatable."

Ally

@FifthHarmony

 camEEla cabeYo @camilacabello97
MARYLAND (and my mother) thank you for the words of encouragement ily a lot

 Normani Kordei @NormaniKordei
#HarmonizeCT !!! YOU GUYS BROUGHT SOOO MUCH ENERGY & WERE SO LOUD I COULDN'T HEAR AFTER LOL BUT THAT'S JUST FINE:)
(to Harmonizers after a concert)

 AllyBrooke Hernandez @AllyBrooke
Billboard Top 100…oh my gosh. Wow. Thank you thank you thank you…to each and every one of you. #DreamsDoComeTrue

 DinahJane @dinahjane97
Today was a day! Love & miss you CHICAGO AND YOUR DELICIOUS PIZZA! #headingtobed #zzzzzzz *(on leaving Chicago)*

Lauren Jauregui @LaurenJauregui
HAPPY ANNIVERSARY GIRLS I LOVE YOU
(on being together as 5H for a year)

NORMANI

Girly-girl ...with a twist!

➤ Normani's style: **Girly-girl ... but with a twist!**

"If I wore a big pink dress, I'd wear it with combat boots ... or I'd wear heels with spikes!"

➤ Normani's favourite accessories:

Quick, put on your shades – here comes sparkly Normani! It's a BLING thing!

"Bling is my no.1 thing! I have to have bling all the time. If I can't have bling, I'm like, 'hmm ok...'"

➤ We've also noticed that...

Normani knows that sometimes less is more – she's one classy girl!

➤ Normani also likes:

Strong patterns and big earrings!

HARMONY HEROES

The Best of British...

Fifth Harmony has a big boy band crush on **One Direction**. "We really love their vibe," says Lauren. "We feel we could be great friends with those boys."

Little Mix is another British group that 5H look up to. "They've really inspired us," says Normani. "It's great to be on the same [record] label as those guys."

And the love goes both ways...

Cher Lloyd was so impressed by 5H after she heard the girls perform one of her songs that she wanted them to go on tour with her... and used Twitter to invite them!

Cher Lloyd @Cherlloyd 🐦
@FifthHarmony Just seen your video and I love it!!! How would you girls like to come on tour with me?xxx(:

Fifth Harmony @FifthHarmony 🐦
OMGGG@CHERLLOYD WE LOVE YOU SO MUCH!!!! CAN WE PLEASE!!

5H inspirations

Ally's biggest influence is the late Tejano music legend, **Selena Quintanilla Perez**. "She is my favourite artist of all time. I loved her so much. Not only did she have an amazing stage presence, a beautiful voice and a vibrant personality, but she also had such charisma and a big heart," Ally says. "She cared for her fans deeply and always showed so much love to everyone. She made me want to become an artist."

The girls all love **Ed Sheeran**, especially Camila who is CRAZY about him. "Fifth Harmony are basically five girls who can sing … a lot!" said Ed at one of his performances. "They covered one of my songs (*Lego House*) and it was very good … that Camila can sing very well." Sounds like Ed likes 5H as much as they like him!

The girls all agree that **Beyoncé** is a big inspiration for them. They were totally overwhelmed when they ended up working with her creative director, Frank Gaston.

"We look up to her so much," said Camila when she introduced **Demi Lovato** for their X Factor duet of *Give Your Heart a Break*. "You're so sweet … I love you guys," said Demi, returning the compliment. And Demi continues to be a massive influence for 5H, along with **Katy Perry, the Spice Girls and Destiny's Child.**

Normani Kordei @Normani Kordei
OMG! I am so crying right now! I can't breathe! Frank Gaston!!! Beyonce's creative director is working with US!!!

FIFTH HARM

CAMILA

5H PROFILE

Name: Camila Cabello

Born: 3rd March 1997

Star sign: Pisces

Hair colour: Brown

Eye colour: Dark brown

Hometown: Miami, Florida

➤ Camila was born in Cuba and moved to the USA when she was just 6 years old. She grew up in Miami which she describes as the 'Cuban homeland'.

➤ Camila is cute and kooky; she loves a joke.

➤ "Teenage girls get caught up with trying to be perfect," says Camila. "Nobody's perfect – everybody's weird whether they embrace it or not!"

Greetings from **FLORIDA** *USA*

"We want to be collectively unique and yet show our individuality."

Camila

Fifth Harmony love ... their Harmonizers

"The best thing about meeting Harmonizers is being able to say 'hi' to them and thank them for their loyalty and dedication as fans." Ally

"Having fans is new to us, we still get sooo excited! When we arrive somewhere and the Harmonizers are waiting, we scream as much as they do!" Camila

"Sometimes we recognize fans from when we've seen them at other events. That's like, so cool!" Dinah

5H Embarrassing moments

Lauren

Lauren was lost for words when she was on a date once. She was having dinner with a guy and when the bill came... "I went for my purse to pay my half, but he was like, 'er, I have no money, could you spot me?' – so I had to pay the whole bill."

Camila

Camila worries about her awkward moves – she once forgot herself during a performance of *Let It Be* and suddenly realized she was doing her own thing instead of dancing in sequence with her girls... Oops! "When I watched it back, I looked so awkward!" she laughed.

5H love...

When the girls want to relax together they go to the movies.

"We go on dates with just the five of us," explained Ally. **"We love to hang out with each other,"** added Lauren.

5H love...

Ally loves her family. **"They are the most important thing to me,"** she says.

5H love...

"My Ray-Ban sunglasses are the most expensive thing I own," says Lauren, **"but the ring my grandma gave me is the most precious."**

Dinah

One time, Dinah was desperate for the bathroom just as Fifth Harmony were about to go on stage to perform *Anytime You Need a Friend* and only just made it in time – perhaps they should have renamed it 'Anytime You Need the Bathroom!'

Hey girls, who said you could write on the wall? Wait ... you're signing an autograph wall at Sirius XM Studios? OK, that's all right then!

STYLE FILE

ALLY

➥ *Ally's style:* **Mummy's Girl**

Ally loves to go to the mall with her mum.

"My mom can put things together in a way I would never have thought of, so I guess I get my style from her."

Ally loves bright neon colours, **"like from the 80s!"**

➥ *Ally's favourite accessories:*

Earrings – big hoopy ones!

➥ *We've also noticed that...*

Ally looks great in shorts – she's got a fine pair of pins!

➥ *Ally also likes:*

Mixing polka dots, stripes and floral patterns!

WHEN THEY WERE YOUNG

5H shine out on stage, but what are these great girls really like when they step out of the spotlight?

When they were young...

Their biggest dream has already come true, but what did 5H want to be when they were little girls?

Normani was a gymnast when she was young and dreamed of making it to the Olympics.

Lauren thought being a doctor would be pretty cool.

"I wanted to be a dentist for a while," says Camila.

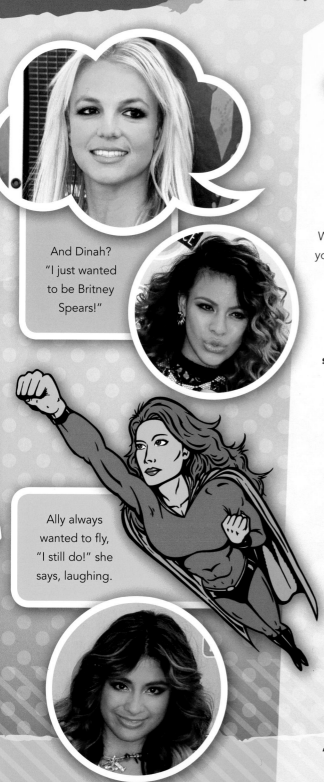

And Dinah?
"I just wanted to be Britney Spears!"

Ally always wanted to fly, "I still do!" she says, laughing.

Special Talents

We all know that 5H are great singers, but did you know they had other amazing talents, too?

Camila

Camila can read freakishly fast – Ally says, **"If you hand her something to read, she hands it back almost right away and I'm like, 'did you read that already?'"**

Lauren

Lauren can type very quickly – *take a letter, Miss Jauregui!*

Normani

Normani can put her legs behind her head. Wow! **"I used to be a gymnast,"** she explains.

Dinah

Dinah has a special talent for hetting mer gords wuddled – er, getting her words muddled! **"And I can burp real well, too!"** she says, proudly.

Ally

Ally has a weird wiggly thumb! **"Whoa – that's crazy!"** says Lauren, when she sees it.

NORMANI

5H PROFILE

Name: **Normani Kordei**

Born: **31st May 1996**

Star sign: **Gemini**

Hair colour: **Dark brown**

Eye colour: **Brown**

Hometown: **New Orleans, Louisiana**

➤ Normani was born in Atlanta, Georgia but grew up in New Orleans. She and her family were forced to move to Houston, Texas when Hurricane Katrina struck in 2005.

➤ Performing from an early age has helped Normani build up her confidence. Naturally rather shy, she fights her fears by giving herself an alter-ego when she's on stage.

> **"We're like one person in five bodies!"**
> Normani

➤ "When I'm on stage I pretend like I'm Beyoncé," confides Normani.

WHO IS THE... ?

Sleepiest?

Definitely **Dinah!** "I like to sleep late," she explains. "She's a very heavy sleeper and we have to shake her to wake her!" adds Normani.

Flirtiest?

"**Ally** is definitely the flirtiest," says Camila. "No, I'm not!" objects Ally. "Well, she's so sweet to everyone; perhaps it just comes off as flirting!" offers Lauren.

Clumsiest?

"That's got to be me!" confesses **Camila**, who often complains that she's too awkward.

Weirdest?

That's **Ally** again! "But only in a cute, kooky kind of way!" explains Dinah. "She's sooo funny!" agrees Normani.

Loudest?

"**Normani** has the loudest laugh you ever heard!" says Ally. "OMG, she'll suddenly just burst out laughing really LOUD!" agrees Camila.

Most sensitive?

That's got to be **Lauren**. "She can always sense if one of us is feeling a little nervous or sad about something," says Ally. "She's like, 'are you all right?' – she can always tell."

Biggest techie?

Dinah is always texting and **Camila** loves the Internet. "I do love being online," she admits.

The girls are walking tall here when they go on a shopping spree at the grand opening of Top Shop, LA. Check out their cool platforms!

CAMILA

➤ *Camila's style:* **Tropical Sunshine Girl**

Being Cuban has influenced Camila's style. She doesn't like jackets and trousers so much.

"I'm more of a shirts and shorts sort of a gal!"

➤ *Camila's favourite accessories:*

Hairbands with cute bows!

Camila never wore heels before being on The *X Factor* and now she's stumbled into a world of heels, make-up and fashion! Long gone are her days of staying in, wearing PJs. Now it's glamour all the way!

➤ *We've also noticed that...*

Camila likes to wear bright lipsticks – it highlights her cute smile!

➤ *Camila also likes:*

Cute collars and sunglasses!

WALK TO STARDOM

Walk our path to fame in this great game of career choices and chances!

START HERE!

You get to sing at the auditions for *The X Factor*. Do you choose to sing?

Someone Like You by Adele

Knew You Were Trouble by Taylor Swift

You get too emotional and your mascara runs. Do you?

Run off stage!

Work with the emotion!

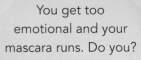

You trip over your feet and find yourself 'lying on the cold hard ground'. Do you?

Bounce back up

Burst into tears

OMG!
You're through to the second round!

You get to duet with a star! Who do you pick?

Beyoncé

Justin Bieber

OUT!

UNBELIEVABLE!
You're in the final!

You are interviewed before your act. You tell the audience to vote...

For you – they must be able to see what a big star you are!

With their hearts – that's what you'll be singing with!

Your microphone doesn't work. Do you?

Carry on even though nobody can hear

Sidle up to Beyoncé and share

2nd

RUNNER UP!
Still good, but watch out for your big head!

When Justin appears you:

Sing together in pefrect harmony

Sing really loud to show him how great you are

WINNER!
You followed your heart and it got you to the top!

OUT!

LAUREN

5H PROFILE

Name: **Lauren Jauregui**

Born: **27th June 1996**

Star sign: **Cancer**

Hair colour: **Brown**

Eye colour: **Green**

Hometown: **Miami, Florida**

➤ Growing up around lots of loud people has given Lauren a lust for life, but finding stardom hasn't gone to her head. "My family is the most important thing to me," she says.

➤ Lauren is an outgoing person and loves to talk to people when she's out and about. On stage she sometimes finds she's lost for words – but luckily she's never tongue-tied when singing!

➤ With its husky quality, Lauren's mature voice is a distinctive element within the group.

Greetings from **FLORIDA** USA

> "We're teenage girls hoping teenage girls can listen to the songs and feel like we're saying what they want to say."
>
> **Lauren**

WHICH FIFTH HARMONY MEMBER ARE YOU?

Answer these questions to find out which 5H member you are most like!

1. What type of clothes do you prefer to wear?

A) You like to be comfy, so shorts and shirts will work best

B) Anything, as long as you can wear it with lots of bling!

C) Something your mum picked out for you

D) Ripped jeans and a tank top

E) A floral dress with a leather jacket

2. Time for some food – what would you choose?

A) Junk food

B) Chicken nuggets

C) Something Mexican

D) Pizza

E) Anything, you're not a fussy eater

3. You're at a party. What will you be doing?

A) Looking for an Internet connection

B) Laughing very loudly

C) Flirting

D) Texting a friend

E) Poppin' your stuff on the dance floor

4. You run away to join the circus. What would you be?

A) A clown

B) An acrobat

C) The ringmaster

D) A juggler of oranges

E) A fortune-teller

5. You are modelling on the catwalk at fashion week. Would you...

A) Trip over and land in a heap

B) Walk elegantly with perfect balance

C) Wear very high shoes

D) Rock the look

E) Strut your funky stuff

Answers:

If you mostly answered **A** then you're most like cute and kooky **Camila**!

If **B** was your most common choice then you are glamorous **Normani**!

If you went for mostly **C's** then you are most like alluring **Ally**.

D's are for **Dinah** – dynamic!

If **E** was your main answer then it's **Lauren** you're most like: easy-going and funky!

Whatever your combination, it's bound to be harmonious!

SPOT THE DIFFERENCE

Can you spot 10 differences between the photos below.

ANSWERS: 1. Logo near Camila's head, 2. Strands of Camila's hair, 3. Frill on Camila's dress, 4. Dinah's necklace, 5. Lauren's dress colour, 7. Normani's zip, 8. Ally's necklace, 9. Ally's neckace, 9. Ally's dress panel, 10. Logo near Ally's head.

DINAH

Urban Chic

➤ *Dinah's style:* **Urban Chic**

Dinah loves Kim Kardashian's style.

"She can throw on some ripped jeans, a tank top and a blazer and look very chic."

Dinah's also into colour-blocking! Look out - she's got some bright clothes and she's not afraid to wear them!

➤ *Dinah's favourite accessories:*

Big earrings and high-heeled shoes!

➤ *We've also noticed that...*

Dinah likes to add bright colour to the tips of her hair!

➤ *Dinah also likes:*

Sequins and animal prints!

THE 'HARMONIZE AMERICA' TOUR

➤ The girls had a busy summer 2013, Harmonizing America coast to coast – from Boston MA to Los Angeles CA and everywhere in between! No wonder their debut single Miss Movin' On was such a great success.

➤ And the misses are still movin' on! Look out, Harmonizers – they might be coming to a town near you!